THE HALIFAX

DECEMBER·6·1917

Ernest Fraser Robinson

Vanwell Publishing Limited

St. Catharines, Ontario

DEDICATION

To Joan Elizabeth Roué

Design: Linda L. Moroz, Angela A. Irvine
Maps: Peter Brown
Cover Photographs: National Archives of Canada

Vanwell Publishing Limited
1 Northrup Crescent
P.O. Box 2131
St. Catharines, Ontario L2R 7S2

Printed in Canada

CONTENTS

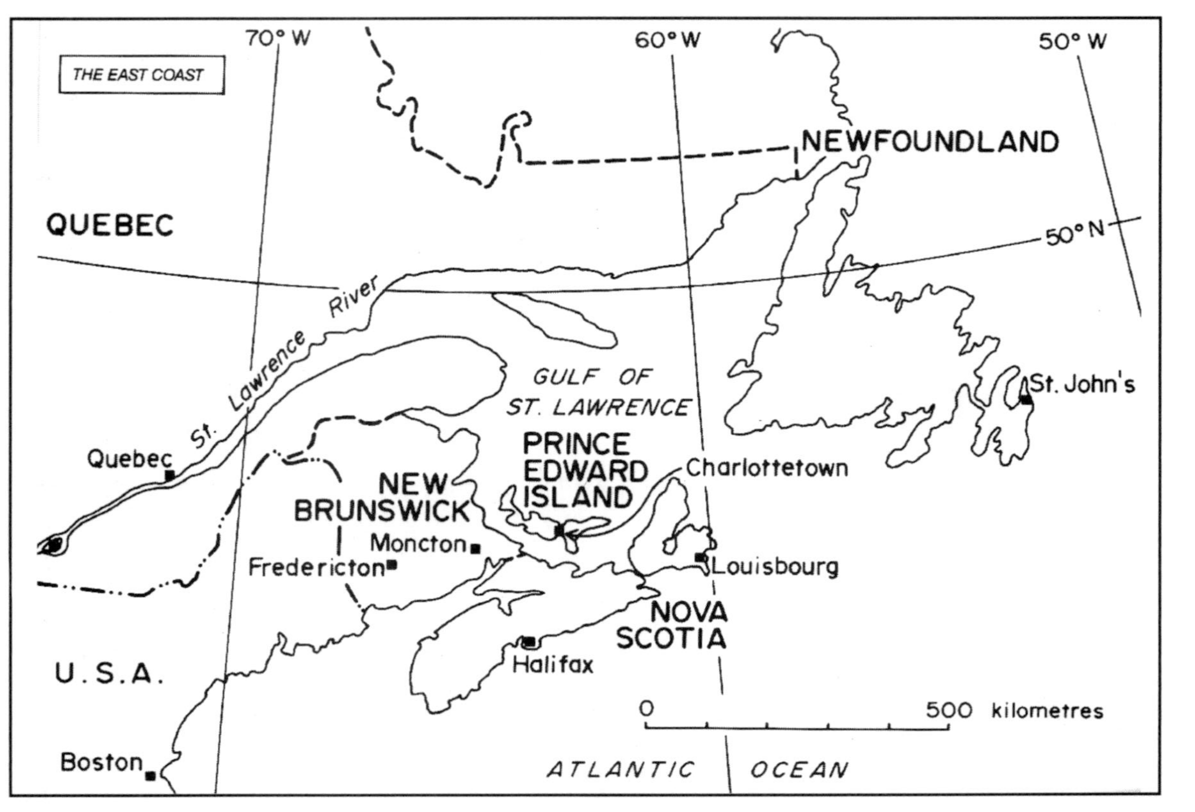
THE EAST COAST
70° W
60° W
50° W
50° N
QUEBEC
NEWFOUNDLAND
St. Lawrence River
GULF OF
ST. LAWRENCE
St. John's
PRINCE
EDWARD
ISLAND
Charlottetown
NEW
BRUNSWICK
Quebec
Moncton
Fredericton
Louisbourg
NOVA
SCOTIA
Halifax
U.S.A.
Boston
0
500 kilometres
ATLANTIC OCEAN

CHAPTER ONE

EAST COAST PORT

On the rugged Atlantic shore of the province of Nova Scotia, about halfway up the coast on one of the world's great natural harbours, lies the port city of Halifax. Before the arrival of settlers from Europe, this place was called "Chebucto", an Indian name meaning "big harbour". To the British, who were fighting a series of wars with the French in the 1700's, Chebucto looked like an ideal location to set up a naval base and fortress. It would increase their power in the North Atlantic, and reduce the threat from the French naval base at Louisbourg, some 350 kilometres northeast, on the island of Cape Breton.

The new base was founded in 1749, and took its name from Lord Halifax, an English nobleman who sent out the first shipload of settlers. Luckily it was his lordship's title rather than his real name, George Dunk, that was used to name the port. Halifax could have been called "Dunktown"!

From its military beginnings, Halifax developed into a major trading port. During the two great wars of this century, it played a vital role in the defense of North America, and in the supply of essential goods to the Allied forces in Europe.

There are a number of unique features which make Halifax a superb harbour for trade or military use. For one thing, the harbour is actually two harbours. The inner harbour, known as Bedford Basin, is about 6 kilometres long and 4 kilometres wide. It provides a perfect haven for all types of ships. During both World Wars, it was in Bedford Basin that ships formed up into convoys to sail to Europe with supplies and munitions.

The main harbour, known as Halifax Harbour, is about 10 kilometres long and almost 2 kilometres wide. Its terminals and docks can service all types of naval and merchant shipping. The inner and outer harbours are connected by a tight channel known as the Narrows. The waters of the harbour reach a depth of fifteen metres, more than enough to handle the largest ships in the world.

The mouth of the harbour is divided by McNab's Island into two channels which are known as the Eastern and Western Passages. The Eastern Passage is too shallow for any shipping other than small fishing boats, and so it is the Western Passage that provides the entrance into the harbour. A narrow bay, the Northwest Arm, lying just to the west of the harbour entrance, extends inland for a distance of about five kilometres. It is suitable for small craft only, and has become a recreational area for sailboats.

The city of Halifax is built on a small triangular-shaped peninsula which lies between the main channel and the Northwest Arm. In the center of this peninsula, rising high above the shore, is a hill which commands a spectacular view of the entire harbour and the ocean beyond. This is the famous Citadel Hill. In the early days of the fortress city, the British set up heavy cannons on the Citadel, making invasion by enemy ships all but impossible. Visitors to Halifax still hear a cannon fired each day from Citadel Hill at 12:00 noon. On special occasions, such as a royal visit, 21-gun salutes are fired.

Beginning with only 1400 settlers in 1749, the seaport grew

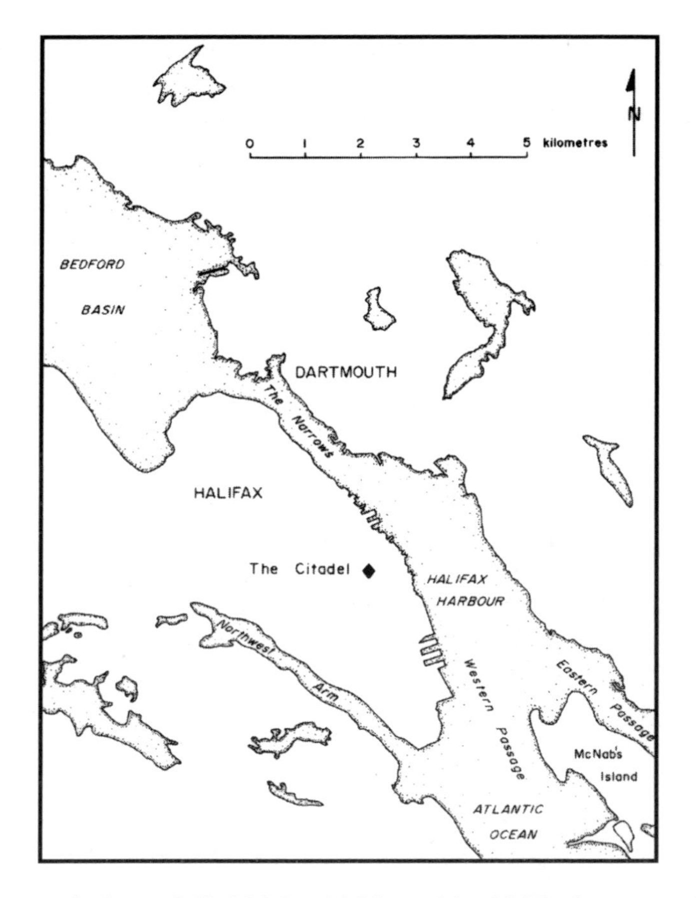

to a population of 40,000 by 1900, and in 1917, the year of the great explosion, the population was about 60,000. Today there are nearly 115,000 residents.

During wartime, Halifax was a very active and prosperous place. Factories hummed as they turned out textiles and various iron and steel products important to the war effort. At the shipyards and in the drydocks, workers set a busy pace to ensure that necessary repairs were made to the ships of war before they left for sea.

Like most seaports, Halifax has seen its share of good and bad times. Those who live close by the sea are a hardy lot who know that nature's way is often stern and unforgiving. They are seldom surprised when bad luck strikes. But even in their nightmares the citizens of Halifax could not have imagined the extent of the devastation which would be brought upon them by a small French freighter called the MONT BLANC.

Halifax from the Citadel, 1888

On December 5, 1917, loaded with a cargo of munitions, the MONT BLANC was slowly making its way through the cold North Atlantic towards the port of Halifax. The captain and crew did not suspect that the MONT BLANC was headed for an appointment with destiny in the Narrows of Halifax harbour.

CHAPTER TWO

THE CITY WAKENS

Thursday, December 6, 1917

Let your imagination take you back in time to the Port of Halifax, Nova Scotia, on that fateful December morning.

An early mist on the harbour has burned away, and the day is going to be clear and bright. Not a cloud is to be seen. There is a slight chill in the air, but hardly any snow lies on the ground. It is just the kind of crisp, fall morning that makes one feel bright and cheery, and ready to take on the duties of the day.

On the waters of the harbour you can see the ferryboat which links the city of Halifax and the town of Dartmouth. It is busy carrying workers back and forth to the foundries and factories which, since the outbreak of war, have been going full out to meet the demands of wartime. Workers at the shipyards and some factories have been on the job since 7:00 a.m. For the most part, they remain completely unaware of anything unusual happening in the harbour this morning.

The city comes awake slowly. By 8:00 a.m. the shops and markets are just beginning to open up for customers. Secretaries, clerical workers, sales clerks, delivery men and others are starting to make their way to their places of employment. There are very few automobiles in 1917, so there are no traffic jams to contend with. Horses and wagons are very com-

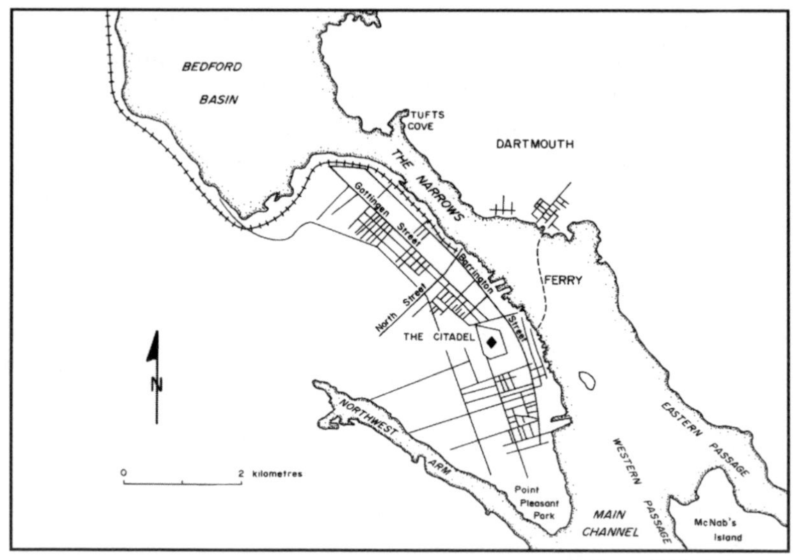

HALIFAX HARBOUR 1917

mon, however, and can be seen moving along Barrington and Gottingen streets and other main routes making deliveries.

Businessmen, and those whose places of business do not open until 9:00 a.m., are lingering over their cups of coffee and their morning newspapers, which are filled with reports on the progress of the war in Europe. School children are finishing their breakfasts, completing early morning chores such as bringing in wood or coal for the kitchen stoves, and getting themselves ready to leave for school. This fall there has been a lot of 'flu' about, and there have even been reports of some children with diphtheria. As a result, school attendance has been down.

At the Richmond Station on North Street, some trains are beginning to arrive. At this station, located near Pier 9, are the freight yards of the Canadian Government Railway. Shortly after 7:00 a.m., a loaded freight train pulls in. The night express train from Saint John, New Brunswick, known as the "Number 10", carrying passengers and mail, is due to arrive around 9:00 a.m., but it is running at least ten minutes late.

At the Royal Naval College of Canada in the Halifax Dockyard, the naval cadets are preparing themselves for their daily duties, including end-of-term examinations for the junior cadets. At the Halifax Armouries and at Wellington Barracks, soldiers are getting themselves ready for the usual morning inspection parades. The city is almost wide awake now, as the pace of activities quickens.

As you cast your eyes over the harbour itself, you will be impressed at the number of things that are going on. Dozens of transports, freighters, and merchant ships are lying at anchor in Bedford Basin, waiting to form a convoy to Europe which is scheduled to leave tomorrow. In the main harbour you can see

Halifax Post Office and Public Market around 1910.

The Halifax Railway Station on North Street around 1900.

tugboats and barges moving busily about, and seamen and longshoremen busily loading and unloading the cargoes of war. Since 1913 the amount of shipping handled by the port of Halifax has increased from two to fifteen million tonnes, making the port one of the busiest in the world.

Some of the ships in the harbour this morning are bound to catch your eye. One is the Belgian Relief ship, IMO. A 4500 tonne ship of Norwegian registry, it is lying at anchor in Bedford Basin and getting ready to leave for New York to pick up relief supplies to go to Belgium. The words "Belgian Relief" are painted in huge red letters on its side to protect it from attack at sea by German submarines. The IMO was supposed to sail last night, but was delayed waiting for 45 tonnes of coal for fuel. Now the coal has been loaded aboard and it is ready to depart.

Halifax harbour around 1917, looking north towards the Narrows. The Acadia Sugar Refinery, smoke rising from its chimney, can be seen at the top left.

Pier 7 in Halifax Harbour around 1917. The Narrows and Bedford basin can be clearly seen. The explosion took place very close to this spot. At left are the Canadian Government railway yards, with workshops and houses beyond.

Anchored in mid-channel is HMS HIGHFLYER, a 5,000 tonne cruiser. This British warship is here to help escort the convoy which leaves for Europe tomorrow. Anchored upstream from HIGHFLYER is HMS CHANGUINOLA, a 5,500 tonne armed merchant cruiser, which will help HIGHFLYER escort and protect the convoy. At the Halifax dockyard is moored HMCS NIOBE, a training ship for the Royal Canadian Navy.

Among the freighters in the main harbour are the PICTON, the CURAÇAO and the CALONNE. The PICTON, a 5,400 tonne freighter moored at the sugar refinery wharf, ran aground on the way to Halifax, damaging its stern post and rudder. This morning a large number of men are at work unloading the general cargo in order to lighten the ship and make repairs easier. While the cargo is chiefly foodstuffs, it is also carrying some high explosives, and the men at work are not allowed to smoke. The CURAÇAO is a fairly new steamship tied up at Pier 8. Loaded with general cargo for Great Britain, it is waiting for a shipment of horses. The SS CALONNE, moored at Pier 9, is also awaiting the arrival of horses for overseas.

Among the harbour tugs to be seen this morning are the LEE, the GOPHER, the MUSQUASH and the DOUGLAS H. THOMAS. The STELLA MARIS, a large ocean-going tug, is at the drydock wharf preparing to tow two heavy barges to Bedford Basin.

One other ship that almost escapes our notice this morning is a small, 2,830 tonne French freighter, the MONT BLANC, just entering the harbour. Last night this ship anchored outside the main channel, waiting for permission to enter. At about 7:30 this morning the MONT BLANC hoisted anchor and began the approach into the harbour. The MONT BLANC is not a ship to attract the eye. Old and tired-looking, it has come to Halifax from New York to join the convoy to Europe.

The MONT BLANC has made many trips across the Atlantic carrying supplies to war-torn France. The Captain, Aimé Le Medec, is known to be a capable and experienced master. The MONT BLANC's cargo, while not unusual for wartime, is nevertheless important and very dangerous. The ship's holds are filled with high explosives. Below decks are stored some 2,100 tonnes of deadly picric acid, a chemical used in the manufacture of explosives, and 200 tonnes of TNT. On the deck itself, in barrels stacked three or four high, are 32 tonnes of highly inflammable benzine. Captain Le Medec rigidly enforces the No Smoking and other safety rules with his crew. He knows that a fire would blow them all sky high. Now, with Captain Le Medec on the bridge, the MONT BLANC carefully eases its way through the harbour entrance.

At the other end of the harbour, at about the same time as the MONT BLANC is entering the main channel, the IMO, the Belgian relief ship moored in Bedford Basin, raises its anchor, and begins to move towards the Narrows, the channel through which it must pass to get into the harbour and out to sea.

It is now approximately 8:15 a.m. For the residents of Halifax and the town of Dartmouth across the water, it has been the start of another normal day. In less than one hour, however, the usual hustle and bustle of the harbour will end in a searing, shattering explosion which will send death and destruction raging in all directions.

CHAPTER THREE

THE COLLISION

Thursday, December 6, 1917
8:45 a.m.

The sea is calm, the sky is clear, the visibility on the harbour is perfect. Not at all the kind of day to expect ships to collide. On board the MONT BLANC and the IMO are experienced harbour guides, or pilots as they are called. They know the many channels in the harbour, and are highly skilled in the methods involved in moving ships to and from the Basin. Only a terrible mistake can lead to an accident on a day so free of the fog and rain which is usual along the coast at this time of year.

Look closely at a map of the harbour, and you will see that the Narrows is a slender passage about 450 metres wide and a kilometre long. As you know, it connects the outer harbour to Bedford Basin~ the sheltered inner harbour which provides a haven for ships that need a quiet place to anchor while waiting their turn to be loaded or unloaded. In wartime, of course, Bedford Basin is a perfect spot for ships to moor before forming up in convoys to sail to Europe.

In tight channels such as the Narrows, it is the rule of the sea that ships having to pass one another will keep to their right, or starboard side. This way they will pass each other on their left, or port side. The MONT BLANC and the IMO, each with an experienced captain and pilot on board, are expected to follow that rule of the sea as they approach one another in the Narrows. Yet, strange as it may seem, the IMO does not follow a normal course at all, and the MONT BLANC will veer sharply from its established course.

Picture the MONT BLANC moving slowly up the harbour, at a speed no faster than four knots. Past McNab's Island it comes, easing over to the starboard side in order to enter the Narrows on the Dartmouth side, exactly as the rules of the sea require ships to do.

Some distance in front of the MONT BLANC is an American tramp steamer headed for anchorage in Bedford Basin. Instead of moving to its right and passing through the Narrows on the starboard side, the steamer stays to the left and enters the Narrows on the port side. By itself, this move by the tramp steamer of course is not so serious. But the Belgian Relief ship, IMO having now made her way through the many ships moored in the Basin, is picking up speed as she approaches the Narrows. What she sees in the Narrows is the tramp steamer on the wrong side. The IMO is forced to move to the left, towards the eastern side of the channel. This is a fateful move, for now both the IMO and the MONT BLANC are moving into the Narrows on the Darmouth side. A collision course has been set.

Even at a distance of a kilometre, Captain Le Medec, standing on the bridge of the MONT BLANC, can spot the IMO entering the Narrows. Imagine his surprise at seeing the IMO coming down at him on the same side. Meanwhile, Captain Brannon of STELLA MARIS, towing two heavy barges into Bedford Basin, sees the IMO in the Narrows. To avoid a collision, Captain Brannon turns his tug back towards the Halifax side of the Narrows, and Captain From of the IMO moves his ship even closer to the Darmouth shore, increasing the risk of collision with the MONT BLANC.

Now a series of whistles echoes back and forth across the harbour, as the ships urgently attempt to signal one another so that each will know the course being followed by the other, as they proceed through the Narrows.

A single blast of the MONT BLANC's whistle splits the air. It is intended to remind the IMO that the MONT BLANC is coming up the Narrows as it should, on the Dartmouth side. Clearly, the MONT BLANC expects the IMO to correct its course and move over to the right side, according to the rules of the sea. This will permit both ships to pass safely. But the IMO replies with two piercing blasts of its whistle, a signal which indicates that it is staying on the present course.

The two ships are now closing on one another so quickly that any steps to avoid collision seem almost too late to try. Nevertheless, the MONT BLANC, in what seems to be a desperate last minute effort, turns sharply to the left. With no room left to pass on the Dartmouth side, the MONT BLANC hopes to cut across in front of the IMO and pass to starboard. At almost the same time the IMO, with three blasts of its whistle, throws the engines into reverse. If these moves work, perhaps they can still miss one another.

Unfortunately, when the IMO reverses its engines it has the effect of swinging the bow of the ship to starboard, directly into the path of the MONT BLANC. With screams of metal grating on metal, and in a shower of sparks, the IMO's bow rips at least 3 metres into the right bow of the MONT BLANC. The metal drums lashed together on the MONT BLANC's deck are torn loose by the force of the impact. The highly flammable liquid benzine spills over the deck and leaks down into the forward holds. The IMO, engines still in reverse, backs slowly away from the MONT BLANC. More sparks fly from the grinding metal. Suddenly the benzine ignites. The MONT BLANC is on fire.

It is now 8:45 a.m.

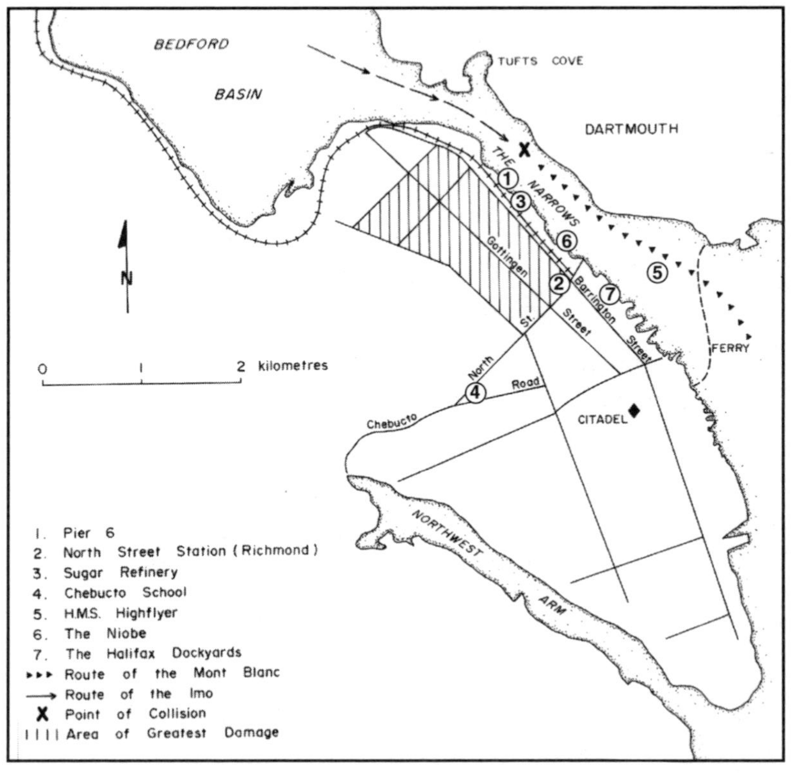

POINT OF COLLISION

4 CHAPTER FOUR

THE EXPLOSION

Thursday, December 6, 1917
9:06 a.m.

Dense clouds of black smoke billow from the deck of the MONT BLANC. They rise 100 metres into the air, and long fingers of orange flame flare up from their base. It is a sight to behold on this bright December morning.

The MONT BLANC, with engines stopped, has enough forward motion to drift slowly towards Pier 6 on the Halifax side of the waterfront. Meanwhile, the IMO, having backed clear of the MONT BLANC, is drifting, but in the direction of the Dartmouth shore. Everything now seems to be happening in slow motion.

All around the harbour, eyes are drawn to the sight of the burning MONT BLANC. In the dockyards and on the wharfs and jetties, men at work look up from their tasks to watch the progress of the fire. Passengers on the morning ferries have a very good view, and from the upper deck they watch what looks to them like an oil tanker on fire. Residents in the Richmond area near Pier 6, whose homes are less than a kilometre from where the MONT BLANC is burning, raise their heads to watch the rising clouds of smoke. Some go upstairs to bedrooms to get a better look from second storey windows. Little do they realize how dangerous a step they have taken. Still, one can imagine the excitement as children and adults call to one another to come up and have a better look at the flaming vessel.

As the MONT BLANC continues to drift slowly towards the piers, the dark smoke from the holds wafts higher into the sky. Children nearing school stop for a long look at the black cloud. Some of them will tarry too long and be directly in line with the force of the explosion when it occurs.

The flat roofs of many buildings along the harbour front are perfect places for spectators to watch what is happening. Tops of buildings such as the Acadia Sugar Refinery next to Pier 6 are filled with interested viewers. Crewmen on the tugboats, and seamen on the various ships at anchor in the harbour, have a clear view of the MONT BLANC, and pause to see the spectacular fire.

On board the MONT BLANC, the crew of forty men is unable to bring the fire under control. Lacking effective means of fighting the flames, they have to stand back as the benzine burns with increasing fury. The fire spreads so quickly that they are unable to do more than watch in horror. Captain Le Medec, realizing that there is no hope of controlling the raging flames, finally gives the order to abandon the ship. Two rowboats are quickly lowered from the side of the doomed vessel, and move off toward the Dartmouth shore, their crews rowing desperately. They know there is little time left for them to reach safety.

Now unmanned, the dying MONT BLANC is almost on top of the wooden pilings at Pier 6. On the pier are stacked a variety of supplies and materials of war which will quickly catch fire if the burning ship strikes. The wooden sheds and storage warehouses built out onto the pier will become raging infernos should they also catch on fire. It is the risk of fire on the docks that has the dockworkers most afraid of what they see happening. They do not know that the fire is the least of the dangers about to confront them.

HMS Highflyer was a British cruiser anchored in mid-channel on Dec. 6, 1917.

The MONT BLANC burns for nearly fifteen minutes before the first fire alarm is sounded. As you can imagine, fire fighting equipment is very simple, nothing like the large fire engines and pumping machines of today. In fact, in Halifax in 1917, there is only one motorized fire engine. The others are horse drawn hose wagons and pumps located in various fire stations across the city. Halifax Fire Chief Edward Condon, on receiving the alarm, immediately sends his new sixty-seven horsepower engine to Pier 6. It is called the "Patricia" and carries a five man crew. Chief Condon and his deputy follow in a car as the "Patricia" races toward Pier 6.

Others also move quickly to bring help to the burning MONT BLANC. The tugboat, STELLA MARIS, leaving its barges at the entrance to Bedford Basin, turns quickly and races back to the distressed vessel. By now the MONT BLANC has rammed into the Pier, setting the wooden pilings on fire. Frantic efforts begin to tie a line to the stern so that it may be towed away from the docks. This action if it succeeds will make it easier to fight the fire on the docks, and will get the MONT BLANC out into the channel where it can do no harm to shipping.

The cruiser, HMS HIGHFLYER, upon seeing the fire break out, sends the ship's whaler, a large rowboat with a crew of seven, to give help. The Canadian training ship, H.M.C.S NIOBE, sends a steam tender, a small supply boat, with sailors ready to give a hand to get the MONT BLANC out into the channel. None of these men are aware of the deadly cargo below the decks of the MONT BLANC. On Pier 9, a warning to run for cover finally is heard. However, it has come much too late to be of any help, and for the men of HIGHFLYER, NIOBE, and STELLA MARIS, struggling to attach a line to the MONT BLANC, it is not heard at all.

Up at the railway yards at Richmond Station on North Street, less than a kilometre from the burning MONT BLANC,

HMCS Niobe, a naval training ship, was moored at the dockyard in Halifax.

HMCS Niobe as refited after the explosion.

is the office of the trian dispatcher. From here, telegraph operator Vincent Coleman issues directions to the various trains entering and leaving the station. At 9:05 a.m., his night shift over, he is ready to leave for home when he recieves a warning about the MONT BLANC. He is told to run for it, but showing great courage, he returns to his telegraph key to send out a final message of warning to incoming trains. "Munitions ship on fire in the harbour," he types out, "Goodbye". These will be his last words.

It is 9:06 a.m. precisely when the MONT BLANC explodes. The ship is blown to bits. The greatest Canadian disaster ever is now happening.

CHAPTER FIVE

THE DAMAGE

What a sight it must have been! Can you picture it in your mind's eye? In a terrific blast of fire and wind, and with a mighty roar that is heard for miles, the MONT BLANC is blown into a million pieces. The scorching heat from the exploding picric acid and TNT turns bits of metal from the ship into red-hot missiles which shoot in all directions, falling in a deadly rain across the city.

A raging wind rips up from the harbour, flattening everything that gets in its way. A huge wave is formed and rushes towards the shore, sweeping away boats and docks before swirling up into the streets. A giant, mushroom-shaped cloud rises several kilometres into the sky, darkening the sun and casting a murky shadow over the stricken city. At first some people believe that Halifax has come under attack by Germans who, from Zeppelins high in the sky, are dropping bombs. But it does not take long for news of the real story to spread.

"Halifax Wrecked. More Than One Thousand Killed," blares the banner headline of the Halifax *Herald* the next day in a handprinted sheet. "All of Halifax north and west of the depot is a mass of ruins, and many thousands of people are homeless." In fact, the damage is much worse than the news-

Site of the Richmond Station (railway), Halifax, after the Halifax Explosion of December 6, 1917.

Nova Scotia's Win-the-War Newspaper

THE HALIFAX HERALD

FOUNDED FEBRUARY 14, 1875. HALIFAX, CANADA, SATURDAY, DECEMBER 8, 1917 VOLUME XLIII, NO

YET MORE APPALLING

The Death Roll Still Grows and the Tremendous Property Loss Is Beginning to be Realized

Sir Robert Borden Offers Federal Aid

SIR ROBERT BORDEN arrived in Halifax yesterday afternoon. The Prime Minister, while in Prince Edward Island heard of the terrible disaster which has overtaken Halifax. He could get no definite information as all means of communication had been cut off by the force of the explosion. Immediately after the meeting at Charlottetown he left for Picton and upon arriving there this morning he at once cancelled his meetings at Antigonish and New Glasgow and started for Halifax by special train, where he arrived late yesterday afternoon in the midst of a tremendous blizzard. He has come to Halifax for the purpose of consulting with the authorities, and of assisting with all the means at the disposal of the federal government, in the arrangements for the relief of those who have suffered so terribly. Naturally he is almost overwhelmed by the magnitude of the calamity to a city with which he has been associated for more than half his life-time, and which he has represented in parliament for more than twenty-one years. One does not feel disposed to engage in political discussion under the shadow of so awful a calamity.

Hon A. K. Maclean spent a great part of the day at the city hall where the various committees were completing organization and directing relief. "It is splendid to see the energy and skill the men and women of Halifax are putting into relief work," said Mr. Maclean to The Herald. "It is in a calamity such as this that the big heart of humankind becomes revealed."

Halifax Will Need Thirty Millions Of Dollars to Meet Situation

Statement by Mr. Justice Harris as Representing the Finance Department of the Citizens Relief Committee.—Food Depots Established at Four Centres for Free Distribution to Stricken Families

HALIFAX, Dec. 8—The following statement is given to the press by Mr Justice Harris, chairman of citizens' finance committee:

"The committee of the citizens of Halifax was appointed to make a public statement on the damage to the city of Halifax and the town of Dartmouth, and after as careful a survey as possible of the damaged area the committee reported that while every building in Halifax and Dartmouth was more or less damaged the devastated area ... near the scene of the explosion and embraces ... districts occupied by workers and the poorer class. Between three and four thousand of such dwellings have been completely destroyed by the explosion or by fire. The number of those affected is estimated at 25,000 ... while of course, the circumstances of all or even most of them cannot be ascertained until each one's case is investigated, yet it is feared that the destitute poor in the area will number upwards of 20,000 and their actual loss and the estimated cost of their temporary maintenance will reach between twenty-five and thirty million dollars. It ... be clearly understood that in this estimate only ... persons rendered destitute are to be considered and ... the portion of the population of Halifax and Dartmouth least able to bear the loss and must be immediately relieved by the generous assistance of their fellow citizens throughout Canada."

Special food depots have been established at four points ... the free distribution of food to all who require it. These are at the City Hall, the Armouries, St. Joseph's and the Cook Construction Company's warehouse. The distribution will be made by baskets to all who apply. The baskets will be made according to the size of the family. Open at the City Hall, the Armouries from 9 a. m. onwards and at St. Joseph's and the Cook Construction Company's from 12.

Dr. Little has opened a FREE dressing station at 94 Gottingen Street.

Found 18 Months Old Child Alive In Debris

HALIFAX, December 8.—Shortly before noon yesterday a squad of seven men of the 63rd, under Sergeant-Major Davies, were at work searching for bodies among the ruins. In a cellar at Richmond they saw a soldier in uniform frantically digging. He called to them for assistance. They found it was Private Henneberry, a former resident of Devil's Island, who had been overseas with a draft of the 63rd and had recently been returned home wounded. "Here was my home," said Private Henneberry, "and I am sure I heard a moan a minute ago." The soldiers listened intently and again came the faint moan of a child in pain. With desperate energy the men dug away the still smouldering debris. Under a stove and protected by the protruding ash-pan, they found little eighteen months' old Olive Henneberry. The child was in a semi-conscious condition. Her mouth was slightly cut and there was a little mark on her face. When taken to Pine Hill hospital she recovered quickly. The lads of the 63rd kept on with the work and found the remains of Mrs. Henneberry, and her five other children.

The Campbell brothers, of Stewiacke, heard the explosion, and realizing that an awful tragedy must have occurred, they came into the city by the first train. Yesterday afternoon they were in the devastated area helping to recover bodies, when they came across a three-year-old boy in a basement and still alive. The little fellow was unconscious, but on being taken to a hospital soon recovered, but was still too dazed to give any statement which would help in his identification.

Save your Glass. There are many Pictures that can go without a Covering and every bit of Glass is Needed

Germans Perilously Near Venetian Plains

LONDON, December 7—In the bloodiest battle yet fought on Italian soil the Germans have won strong Asiago positions with a great bag of prisoners. The guns of Boroevic shifted their tactics, the whole force being concentrated on a ten mile front. The Teutons are perilously near the Venetia plains.

British Withdraw From Bourlon Wood

BRITISH HEADQUARTERS IN FRANCE, ... The British have withdrawn from ... Bourlon wood ... make their positions much stronger and more defensible in many ways. The retirement was carried out successfully mainly early Wednesday morning, and under cover of darkness. Not until many hours later did the enemy discover that he was firing on evacuated territory.

War Declared on Austria

WASHINGTON, December 7.—With less than an hour's debate the senate today passed the resolution declaring war on Austria-Hungary.

AT 3:45 ON THE AFTERNOON OF THE EXPLOSION A DOMINION ATLANTIC TRAIN BROUGHT 45 TRACKMEN AND BRIDGEBUILDERS. THE SAME TRAIN BROUGHT DOCTORS AND NURSES FROM KENTVILLE, WOLFVILLE AND WINDSOR. IT WAS THE FIRST RELIEF TO ARRIVE.

MOTHER AT EIGHTY-ONE

Soldiers Cease Not to Search For Bodies of the Dead Now Numbering 2,000

Scenes of Pathos and Sorrow ... Mothers and Fathers Seek ... Children, and Orphans Refuse to be Comforted Because ... Parents Who Are Not

The Cause of the Catastrophe

Front page from the Halifax *Herald*, Dec. 8, 1917.

paper knows. It will be weeks, even months before the full extent of the losses can be set out in a complete record.

The north end of the city is totally devastated, and heavy damage occurs for miles in all directions. Hardly a house in Halifax or Dartmouth escapes without some damage. Piers and sheds on the waterfront closest to the explosion simply vanish. All that remains are chunks of timber and loose pilings floating on the harbour. Deadly showers of glass and bricks spray everywhere, doing enormous damage and causing many deaths. Hundreds of people are buried alive under buildings which have collapsed. Numerous fires break out in the heavily damaged north end, seriously slowing the rescue work.

Although the MONT BLANC has been blown from the face of the earth, some parts of the ship turn up later on. The forward gun, for example, is found on the Dartmouth side near

The SS Imo aground on the Dartmouth shore. Armed Guards stand watch against looters.

Albro Lake, some three kilometres from the site of the explosion. A piece of the ship's anchor is found on the far side of the Northwest Arm.

The Belgian Relief ship, IMO, takes the blast head on. The bridge and decks are hit hard, and the ship is driven across the harbour where it runs aground on the Dartmouth shore. Seven crewmen on her deck, including Captain From, are killed instantly. STELLA MARIS, the tug which was next to the MONT BLANC when the explosion came, is lifted right out of the water and thrown up on the shore near Pier 6. Captain Brannon and his entire crew are killed outright. Both HMS HIGHFLYER, and HMCS NIOBE suffer severe damage to their decks and have men killed and injured. Still, they are able to send some of their crew ashore to assist in fighting fires and helping the injured. All of the men on the whaler sent by HIGHFLYER to help the MONT BLANC are killed in the explosion, as are all the sailors sent from the NIOBE.

The CURAÇAO, tied up at Pier 8, is torn away from its moorings and is blown across the Narrows into Tufts Cove where it sinks. Most of the crew are killed. The merchant ship, CALONNE, suffers major damage as does the steamer PICTON. The longshoremen unloading cargo from the PICTON's hold perish instantly. Their bodies are strewn across the deck, stripped of clothing by the force of the blast. Black, oily soot raining down from the clouds of smoke, covers them from head to toe. More than a dozen merchant ships are badly damaged by the explosion. A number of harbour tugs, their hulls broken by flying metal, are put completely out of commission.

The fire engine, "Patricia", with its crew of five, having raced at full speed to Pier 6 to try to put out the fire on the MONT BLANC, has hardly managed to get its hose unrolled from the reel when the explosion comes. All but one of the fire-

Halifax's new fire engine, the Patricia, shown after the explosion. Note the broken steering wheel. All of her crew, except the driver, were killed instantly.

men are killed outright, as are Fire Chief Edward Condon and his deputy who were in a car close behind the "Patricia".

A powerful wave, nearly four and a half metres high rises up in the harbour. Racing towards shore, it tears up piers and rips out pilings, smashes tugs and small craft against wharves, and rips larger ships from their moorings. It washes up over the lower streets in the north end of the city and, rushing back into the harbour, carries hundreds of workers and seamen to their deaths.

Such is the force of the explosion that rocks are actually torn from the bottom of the harbour and thrown high into the air.

Dropping back onto the city, they cause much damage. More deadly are the tens of thousands of red-hot metal bits from the MONT BLANC's hull. Falling from the sky like raindrops in a heavy shower, they instantly kill or maim those who are directly hit.

In the north end railway yards, the blast tosses freight and passenger cars around like toys. Heavy steam locomotives are upended and thrown across the yard. Iron rails are ripped from their tracks and bent out of shape as though they were paper straws. The glass roof of the North Street Station collapses onto the platform below. In an instant the whole area is turned into a pile of twisted wreckage and scattered debris. Scores of railway workers are killed, many by the deadly bits of glass and the chunks of hot metal hurtling through the air.

Richmond Station. Many were killed when the roof collapsed.

At the Halifax Drydocks over one hundred workers are killed outright, and scores of others are maimed for life, some of them blinded, some missing an arm or a leg, some missing both. The sugar refinery next to Pier 6 simply crumbles into a heap of bricks and burning timbers. Those workers who earlier had gathered on the roof of the refinery to watch the MONT BLANC as it burned, are torn to bits or just blown away, with no trace of their bodies ever to be found.

The worst damage is done in the Richmond area in the north end of the city. Located near the sugar refinery, and not far from Pier 6 where the MONT BLANC explodes, Richmond is a residential area, built up with homes owned by workers at the shipyards, factories and foundries. They are modest homes, nearly all of wooden frame construction, heated by coal and wood-burning stoves and furnaces. These homes are not strong enough to withstand the terrible force of the blast.

An area of about two square kilometres in Richmond is totally wiped out. Hardly a house remains standing. The streets are so filled with wreckage and rubble, that workers rushing back into the area to learn the fate of their families, are not able to recognize where their homes once stood. Entire families are instantly killed by the blast, their bodies torn beyond recognition.

Hundreds of women and children are trapped in their homes, as roofs and upper floors collapse upon them. Alive, and sometimes not even injured, they will not survive because of the fires which break out following the explosion. The force of the blast upsets scores of coal and wood stoves which had just been fired up for the usual morning household activities. It does not take long for the burning fuel to ignite flames in the dry wooden rubble.

Buried beneath the timbers of their own homes, the women and children burn to death. It is almost too horrible to think about. Rescuers make desperate attempts to reach the victims, but flames and smoke beat back their heroic efforts. A cloud of grey smoke from the smoldering fires in Richmond hangs over the city for hours.

Unaware of what has actually happened, and knowing only that the whole world seems to be exploding around them, scores of panic-stricken residents race out into the streets.

With blood pouring from terrible wounds caused by flying glass and metal, many scream out in their fear and pain. Torn and blinded, their faces black from the oily soot raining from the sky, they run desperately away from the scene, searching for safety and help. The streets in the north end are littered with corpses. Twisted and torn from being thrown violently into the air, many bodies have had all their clothing ripped off before falling lifelessly back to earth.

Hundreds of school children perish in the blast, some sitting at their classroom desks, others at home or on their way to school. In winter, starting time for the children in the lower grades is not until 9:30 a.m., and so most of these students are just setting out when the MONT BLANC explodes at 9:06 a.m. Two hundred children are reported killed at the Protestant Orphanage on Campbell Road, and many others are severely injured by flying glass and debris. Heavy losses of life occur at Richmond and St. Joseph's Schools, and at Roome Street School half the children die. Most of the school buildings in Richmond and in North Dartmouth are so badly damaged that they remain closed for weeks. Nearly every school has some damage, especially to windows.

Tearing across the city dealing death and destruction, the shock waves reach Citadel Hill and bounce upwards. This is truly fortunate because the great force of the blast is weakened, saving the homes in the south end of the city from the heavy damage that was done in Richmond. Windows are broken everywhere. Doors are forced in, and walls and chimneys crack. But very few people in the area are seriously hurt.

Similarly, in the west end, loss of life is not high, but buildings suffer serious damage, and some homes are so badly smashed that they cannot be lived in. In the central business section of the city no buildings are actually demolished, but

All that was left of the Sugar Refinery building.

A view of the north end, looking towards Pier 6 and the Sugar Refinery wharf. The Imo can be seen aground on the Dartmouth side.

there is a lot of damage, and several hundred people are severely injured by flying glass and metal fragments. All the windows are blown in at most of the banks and shops along Barrington, Hollis and other downtown streets.

Across the harbour in Dartmouth the force of the blast is also at its worst in the north end, an area known as Tufts Cove. Many people suffer serious injuries, but there is not the heavy loss of life experienced in the Richmond area. Less than fifty deaths are reported in the whole Dartmouth area. Physical damage, however, is great. Many buildings are totally destroyed by the blast, and scores of people left homeless.

Section showing damage to buildings not burned, looking west.

In the midst of these terrible events, a rumour begins that a second explosion is about to occur. At Wellington Barracks in the north end, a powder magazine is reported on fire.

Everywhere people are warned to find safety in open areas. Panic spreads like wildfire, and thousands flee southward towards Point Pleasant Park and to the open fields of the

Commons behind the Citadel. The additional hardship and suffering can hardly be imagined. Rescue operations are delayed, and many injured are left to die in the burning ruins. We will never know how many lives are lost that might have been saved had this false news not been spread. By noon it is clear that a second explosion will not occur, but the damage has been done.

Of course all the regular services in the city come to a total stop. Telephones are out of order everywhere, and weeks will pass before full service can be restored. All public transportation ceases. Any available vehicles, including horses and wagons, are immediately pressed into rescue work. Getting the injured to hospitals and first-aid centers, and collecting the hundreds of dead bodies are the most urgent activities in these first hours after the blast. Gas mains, water pipes and other city services are out of order. All delivery services, including food and milk, are at a standstill.

It is estimated that nearly twenty-five thousand persons are without shelter following the explosion, and more than six thousand are known to have had their homes totally demolished. Property damage caused by the blast is estimated at $35 million (in today's dollars that would be $451 million or almost half a billion!).

As if the explosion has not inflicted enough damage on the unfortunate city, now Mother Nature unleashes her fury to add to the misery. A full blown blizzard moves into the area on the morning of December 7th, and over the next twenty-four hours rescue work is paralyzed as gusting winds pile snow into heavy drifts, making streets impassable. When the blizzard ends on the next day, the city is hit by a rainstorm which turns the streets to slush. Freezing temperatures follow, creating icy conditions which continue to hamper the clean-up and slow the return of basic services. As you can well imagine, the

Destroyed home after the Halifax explosion.

The north end of Barrington Street. The entire area was as bleak and barren as a battlefield in France.

hardships faced by rescuers and victims alike are enormous.

The official count by the Halifax Relief Commission lists 1,963 persons killed and 9,000 injured in the explosion. Some who have studied the event, think these figures are on the light side. They believe that if all those who disappeared without a trace, and all those killed on board ships in the harbour are included in the count, then the number actually dead is nearer to 3,000. The explosion is the worst disaster in Canadian history, and the most devastating man-made explosion ever, until the atomic bombs are dropped on Japan in 1945.

CHAPTER SIX

THE STRUGGLE TO SURVIVE

Now, in the quiet that follows the blast, thousands of injured, many in terrible pain from their severe wounds, descend upon the hospitals. Compared to the modern, well-equipped buildings we are used to, these hospitals are small and very limited in the medical services they are able to offer. Working with equipment, medicine and drugs not nearly as advanced as we know today, the doctors and nurses begin their struggle to care for the victims. In the next few days they must face conditions beyond anything they thought possible.

Since there are hardly any motorized ambulances, and because many of the horse-drawn vehicles have been damaged or destroyed in the blast, the wounded arrive by any means available to them. Some stagger in on foot, while others are hauled or pushed to the hospital doors on flat wagons, coal carts and even wheelbarrows. The few motor cars available in the city are quickly taken over to serve as ambulances. Some owners offer to drive their own cars, while others simply turn their cars over to the Army. But a few do not seem to understand how serious the situation is, and must be forced to give up their cars.

COPY OF TELEGRAM FROM HIS MAJESTY KING GEORGE V.

TO THE GOVERNOR GENERAL.

Buckingham Palace.

8th December 1917.

Most deeply regret to hear of serious explosion at Halifax resulting in great loss of life and property. Please convey to people of Halifax where I have spent so many happy times my true sympathy in this grievous calamity.

(Sd.). GEORGE R. I.

Looking for bodies at the Railway Station.

The rescue parties put every available vehicle to use to move the wounded. Soon every hospital in the city is filled to overflowing. Some patients have to lie outdoors on makeshift stretchers until room for them can be found in the crowded wards and corridors. Emergency treatment centers are set up across the city in parish halls, church basements, theatres, and in local Y.W.C.A. and Y.M.C.A. buildings. Medical supplies, including anesthetics and bandages are soon in short supply, a situation which improves with the arrival of medical relief trains from outside the city.

Rescue operations get underway soon after the explosion. At first, it is the survivors themselves who team together to pull victims from the smoking wreckage. They manage to get many of the wounded on carts which will transport them to the hospitals. Rescue teams arrive from the NIOBE and HIGHFLYER and other naval ships in the harbour. The military garrisons send teams of soldiers to rope off damaged areas, and to lead

Children getting food supplies at a relief station.

rescue efforts. Military patrols are put on the streets to keep law and order, and to prevent looters from entering the damaged stores and commercial buildings.

There is real danger from the spreading fires, and the fire department struggles bravely throughout the day to bring them under control. By late afternoon, the worst of the danger is over, but under the massive piles of debris, small fires continue to burn for days.

Hundreds of people are without shelter of any kind. Soldiers from the local garrisons work to erect temporary shelter for the homeless on the north commons. Citizens whose homes have not been severely damaged are quick to offer room. Emergency relief stations are set up as quickly as possible at various locations across the city. Supplies of food, blankets and clothing are issued to the victims, some of whom have lost absolutely everything. Soup kitchens are opened up to provide on-the-spot food to the cold and hungry.

A search party forms up to look for survivors.

Soldiers engaged in rescue work in Halifax, N.S. after the disaster.

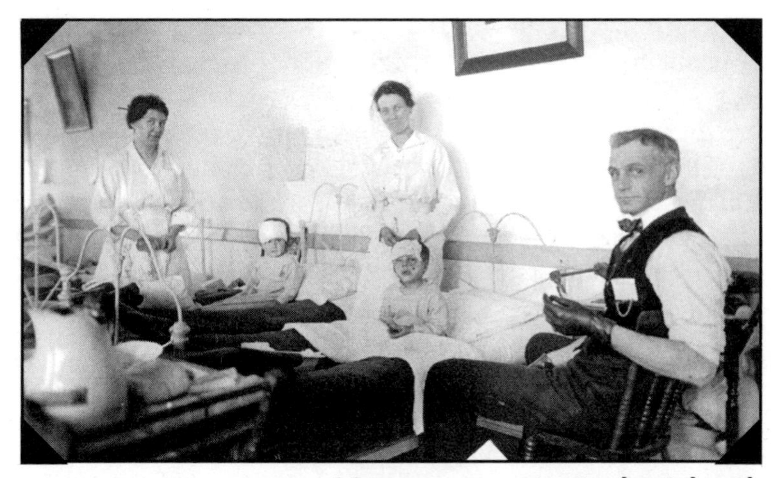

A Doctor treats a patient in a hospital ward.

Children's party at a temporary hospital.

Other teams are sent out to collect the bodies of the dead. For health reasons and for identification, it is essential that the corpses, many badly cut and torn, be brought to one spot and have tags attached to them. These tags have information such as where the body was found, and other details to help with identification later on. One location for the keeping of bodies until identification is made is the basement of Chebucto Road School. For those assigned to work there, it is a grisly but necessary task.

Although telephone lines have been virtually wiped out, a telegraph link is still working, and word of the terrible disaster quickly spreads to the outside world. Among the earliest to respond to the call for help, are two American vessels, the U.SS VON STEUBEN and the U.SS TACOMA, which arrived in port shortly after the explosion. Both of these ships are quick to send working parties ashore to help in rescue work. Another American ship, the OLD COLONY, is pressed into service as a hospital ship, relieving some of the pressure on the hospitals in the city.

A relief train carrying doctors, nurses and medical supplies arrives from Kentville, about one hundred kilometres away, at 12:30 in the afternoon. It can get no farther than Rockingham, on the outskirts of Halifax, and the doctors are forced to walk the rest of the way in. One of the doctors reports seeing a roadway with dead bodies piled up several feet high, like cordwood. Such sights are not unusual.

Over the next few days, several trains arrive with much needed assistance for the bruised and bleeding city. From Boston and New York come special trains laden with medical supplies, hospital equipment, and doctors and nurses. Other supplies include hundreds of cots and several thousand blankets, as well as food and clothing. A steamship from Boston brings glass and construction materials to help in the rebuilding. The Red Cross in New York is able to arrange for the shipment of a large quantity of anti-pneumonia serum. The Americans are quick and generous in their assistance to the wounded city.

The Government of Canada provides nearly $20,000,000 in aid, and other pledges of money come from Great Britain, New Zealand and Australia. Hundreds of cities and towns across Canada raise money which is forwarded to the Halifax Relief Commission to help in the rebuilding of the city. In total, nearly $30,000,000 is raised.

As soon as the railway tracks are cleared of debris, special medical trains leave Halifax for nearby centers such as Truro and Windsor to lighten the crowded conditions in the city hospitals.

Nature does not make the rescue operations at all easy. Winter storms lashing the coast hinder the efforts to find victims and clear the wreckage. Words can hardly describe the terrible suffering. And to that suffering must be added the agony of those who themselves survive, but lose loved ones, sometimes entire families. Nor can we ever know the many acts of individual heroism and sacrifice that have taken place in the hours that followed the blast.

7 CHAPTER SEVEN

THE EYE-WITNESSES

As you would expect, many first-hand accounts have been given over the years by those who vividly remember what they saw and experienced on the day of the explosion.

Billy Wells, the only survivor from the crew of the fire engine "Patricia", was able years later to recall in detail what happened to him.

"I was the driver", he said, "and we immediately rushed down to the pier. The ship was almost alongside the dock and the multi-coloured flames shooting from its decks presented a beautiful sight. The first thing I remember after the explosion," he continued, "was standing quite a distance from the fire engine. The force of the explosion had torn off all my clothes as well as the muscles of my right arm."

Then came the large wave which washed up over the piers crushing everything in its path.

"After the wave had receded," he said, "I didn't see anything of the other firemen so made my way to the old magazine on Campbell Road. The sight was awful, with people hanging out of windows dead. Some with their heads off, and some thrown onto the overhead telegraph wires. I was taken to Camp Hill Hospital and lay on the floor for two days waiting for a bed."

Another interesting account is that of W.J. McCall, who was a Grade 4 student at Park School in Dartmouth. He was in his classroom that morning when the MONT BLANC exploded.

"It was 9:05 a.m. and we had just finished singing our good morning tune and God Save the King. We got seated when wham! - and the old brick chimney came right down the aisle beside me. How most of us in that old classroom escaped the flying bricks and glass was an amazing thing in itself."

Other members of Mr. McCall's family also had a narrow escape. "My mother and younger brother David escaped serious injury or possible death that day because they were called outside our Fairbanks Street home to look at the ship burning in the harbour. They hadn't gone far when the explosion occurred and both were tossed as if scooped up by a giant lift, high over old oak trees near the corner of Best Street. Both were untouched by the hail of flying metal in the air around them and were wafted like feathers in a breeze and finally deposited on the street. Their survival like that of many others involved in similar incidents was miraculous..."

A similar story of escape from death was told shortly after the explosion by Third Officer Mayers of the SS MIDDLETON CASTLE, a merchant ship moored some 180 metres from the MONT BLANC when she blew up. Mayers had just come on deck, and was preparing to go ashore on business when the blast occurred.

The newspaper reporter who interviewed Mayers wrote as follows: "Mayers was lifted into the air by the shock of the blast and at some height driven through the air at such terrific speed that he tried, in vain, to check it. He says he remembers being in the air all right, though while there thought at first he was going through water, and hence his efforts to check his speed. Though fully dressed when lifted from the deck, Mr.

The SS Calonne was badly damaged. To her left can be seen the stern of the tug Hilford. The force of the explosion threw her right out of the water.

Mayers says he was stark naked when he landed well up on Fort Needham Hill, and he was convinced he was carried the distance of almost a kilometre or more through the air by the force of the explosion."

Fred Longland, a sailor attached to HMCS NIOBE, gave an account of the effect of the explosion on his ship.

"What an unholy mess the main deck was in; 19 men lay dead without a mark of any kind on them and the wounded crowded the sick bay for attention."

He recalled the scene in the harbour: "Cargo ships partially wrecked, drifted about out of control ... A large tugboat was reposing on No. 2 Pier dropped there by the tidal wave. Four large cargo ships were complete wrecks with their middles cut out as though by a great scythe. I was detailed now to take a platoon and look for dead sailors on the streets, and in the schools which had been turned into morgues. The bodies just as they were picked up, were in the boys' side of the school, and when cleaned up a bit were laid out in the girls' side for identification."

Edward McCrossan was a member of the crew of the freighter CURAÇAO who, fearing that some ammunition on his ship might explode, went ashore near Pier 9 shortly after the MONT BLANC blew up. Later he told his experiences to a newspaper reporter. "We clambered up on the wreck of the pier and found a soldier standing there who had been on duty. Part of his right jaw had been blown off. I asked him what was the quickest way to get out and he said he didn't know and that he felt half dead. He asked me if I would help him get rid of his gear. I took his belt and pouches off and threw them into the water and told him he could always get more of these. His overcoat was torn in ribbons. He wanted me to help him along,

A public funeral for the unidentified dead from the morgue at Chebucto School.

and we climbed over some sort of a wrecked wooden building and up to the railway track. By this time we could see the houses all afire and could see the women and children rushing out screaming and crying. A lot of them were covered in blood. I saw one woman with two holes through her face and smothered in blood and I said to the soldier: 'Mate, you better make the best of your way along the track and I'll see what I can do to help this woman'. The woman was crying and kept saying that she was dying."

J.C. MacKeen, a Halifax businessman, worked tirelessly in rescue operations. "I acquired a team consisting of two sailors, a soldier and myself, and for a stretcher we got a piece of picket fence. We rolled back the top of the car and went into the burning area and rushed the victims to the new Camp Hill Hospital.

The small public square at the head of Young Street and Gottingen Street was being filled up by the dead and wounded, brought up as could be managed from the wrecked and burning buildings. There was no difficulty in filling the car, load after load, as quickly as possible, and taking them to the nearest hospital."

He also recalled that "Many families became separated and the frantic search for young children started. By and large, however, the large mass of the population who had been close to the explosion were numb with a species of shellshock and they kept wandering aimlessly about."

Doctor W.B. Moore of Kentville, who had come down on the first relief train at noon on the day of the explosion, recounted the horrors which greeted the doctors. "Many of us had seen terrible sights of human tragedies and suffering but nothing like this ... Men, women, and children of all sorts and classes were literally packed in the wards like sardines in a box, the cots all occupied, and the floors covered so that it was often difficult to step between them. The ghastly appearance of so many ... was really trying ... and some of the men who had been at the front in the war declared that they had never witnessed anything so terrible."

Hundreds of such personal stories can be told, all of them bearing stark witness to the horror of that December day in Halifax. None, perhaps, is more likely to bring a tear to one's eye, than that to be found in one of the many official reports giving details of the care provided for the wounded and dying. It is a sad story about a little, three-year old girl who had to have both her eyes removed. As she recovered consciousness after the operation, she is reported to have clapped her hands with pleasure and happily said to her nurse, "Oh, Nurse, it's night, isn't it?"

CHAPTER EIGHT

THE BLAME

Who was to blame for the explosion? In the days after the blast, demands grew to find out where the fault lay, and to punish the guilty. Everyone knew the collision should not have occurred. Was it just carelessness? Did one or both of the ships fail to follow the rules on passage? Was it an act of sabotage by German spies? At first there were many who thought so, and feelings against the Germans were very strong. It is said that some residents of the city with German backgrounds, or German sounding names, were badly treated. Beatings were reported, and some homes were attacked. But such views were not held for long, since no proof at all could be found to support them.

Hearings on the cause of the explosion began on December 13 at the Halifax Court House on Spring Garden Road. Among the witnesses called were Captain Le Medec of the MONT BLANC, and his pilot, Francis Mackey, and some of the surviving crew members of the IMO. Another important witness was Commander Frederick Wyatt, the naval officer in charge of the movement of all large vessels in the harbour.

Captain Le Medec and Pilot Mackey held firm to their story that the MONT BLANC stayed in its correct channel all the way up the harbour, and that it was the course taken by the I MO that caused the collision. Lawyers for the IMO took the opposite view, arguing that there would have been no collision at all had the MONT BLANC not veered across the IMO's bow.

The Commission made its report on February 14, 1918, and laid the blame entirely on Captain Le Medec, Pilot Mackey and Commander Wyatt. In spite of all the evidence to the contrary, the Commission said that the MONT BLANC did not follow the correct course as the rules of the sea required. It recommended that Pilot Mackey be fired, and that the French Government be asked to cancel Captain Le Medec's license to sail. It also ruled that Commander Wyatt was guilty of negligence for failing to properly control the movement of ships in the harbour.

All three men were arrested on charges of manslaughter. However, the charges did not stand up in court and were soon dropped. Captain Le Medec and Pilot Mackey were cleared of any guilt.

The owners of the MONT BLANC sued the owners of the IMO for $2,000,000 in damages. The case was heard in the Supreme Court of Canada and the court ruled that both ships were equally to blame for what happened. An appeal to the court of the Privy Council in London resulted in a similar decision. The ruling this time stated that the MONT BLANC did stay in its proper course, and that the IMO could have avoided the collision. However, the court also said that the pilots of both ships allowed themselves to get too close, making a collision unavoidable. Francis Mackey returned to his job as a harbour pilot, and Captain Le Medec served as a ship's captain for many years after. The case was finished.

HALIFAX
- Today -

Top: Halifax harbour today showing ferry coming towards Dartmouth.

Bottom: Modern deep sea oil drilling rigs at anchor near the Eastern Passage of Halifax harbour.

Top: Restoration of the Historic Properties along the Halifax harbour front.

Bottom: A recent photograph which looks across the Narrows from Tufts Cove. This is the area in which the collision between the Imo and the Mont Blanc took place.

IN REMEMBRANCE

This poem, which was printed in the *Halifax Mail-Star* newspaper on the occasion on the 50th anniversary of the Halifax Explosion, was written by one of the survivors.

The Halifax Disaster

It was on the sixth of December
Nineteen hundred and seventeen,
Halifax suffered disaster
The worst she had ever seen.

The morning was bright with sunshine
A typical winter day.
None had thought of danger
As they wandered their busy way.

The children had gone to their lessons
Their mothers were busy at home,
While fathers worked in factories
Little dreaming they'd soon be alone.

There comes creeping up the harbour
A ship loaded down in the rail,
With the most horrible death dealing cargo
That was ever allowed to sail.

She carried a deck load of benzol
And shells for overseas,
In her hold a new explosive
They called it TNT

Now why should this death dealing monster
Be allowed to come creeping up here,
To bathe our beautiful city
In widow and orphans' tears.

The relief ship rammed the monster
Tearing a hole in her side,
Then eased out in the stream again
And drifted along with the tide.

There came a cry from a merchant
"There's a steamer on fire out there!"
But few paid any attention
As that is the fireman's care.

It was five minutes after nine
As those still alive can tell,
The beautiful city of Halifax
Was given a taste of Hell.

The earthquake hath its rumble
The cannon hath its roar,
But this was worse than even those
Yes, multiplied by four.

And when the crash was over
Those still alive struck dumb,
Turned into living statues
And wondered what next would come.

For no one knew what had happened
Some thought it the end of the world,
And others thought 'twas Germans
Marching in with banners unfurled.

Then rushing forth into the streets
From their tumbling and shattered homes,
Some with cuts and bruises
And others with broken bones.

They were met by a sight more horrible
Than any there had been,
For there lay the dead and dying
'Twas worse than a battle scene.

Houses were crushed like paper
The people were killed like flies,
And the coroner's record tells us
The toll was a thousand lives.

From north to Rockhead Hospital
   And west to the exhibition ground,
There wasn't anything living
   And not a single sound.

The streets were filled with debris
   With dying and with dead,
There lies a little baby's hand
   And there's an old man's head.

There out upon the Common
   That cold December morn,
Tender little innocent souls
   Into this world were born.

Women hugged their children
   Their hearts were filled with fear,
While husbands lay beneath the homes
   They all had loved so dear.

And on the following morning
   As if to hurt them twice,
There came a storm from the ocean
   A blizzard of snow and ice.

Freezing the poor unfortunates
   Who had no place to go,
And many a poor soul
   Drifted to heaven from out of the snow.

The States weep with you, Halifax
   In this your hour of sorrow,
They offer you their help and gold
   So don't wait 'til tomorrow.

But step right up and help yourself
   And We the bill will pay
For that's the way they do things
   In the good old U.S.A.

READING & RESOURCE MATERIALS

BOOKS

Bird, M.J. *The Town That Died*. Souvenir, 1962.

Borrett, W.C. *More Tales Told Under The Old Town Clock*. Imperial Publishing Company, 1943.

Garrison, W *Disasters That Made History*. Abingdon, 1973.

Metson, G. (ed.) *The Halifax Explosion, December 6, 1917*. McGraw-Hill Ryerson, 1978.

McLennan, H. *Barometer Rising*. Duell, 1941.

Monnon, M.A. *Miracles and Mysteries*. Lancelot Press. 1977.

PERIODICALS

"After the Blast". *Time* Magazine (Canadian Edition). February 24, 1975.

Gilligan, E. "Death In Halifax". *Reader's Digest*. March, 1938.

Taylor, R. "A City Destroyed". *Canada And The World*. May, 1975.

Waller, A. "Explosion!". *Reader's Digest*. (Canadian Edition). December, 1977.

Signs on boarded up store front asking for help.

INDEX

ABOUT THE AUTHOR

ERNEST FRASER ROBINSON

Ernest Fraser Robinson was born in Cape Breton, Nova Scotia. A retired teacher, he now divides his time between his home in Burlington, Ontario and his summer home in North Hatley, Quebec.

PHOTOCREDITS

National Archives Canada (NAC) C9390 p. 8 NAC C 19265 p. 11, Photo by Notman Studio, Nova Scotia Archives p. 12, PANS Collection (upper) Nova Scotia Archives p. 13, Photo by Gauvin Gentzel (lower) Nova Scotia Archives p. 13, Reproduced from Jane's Fighting Ships 1911 by Fred T. Jane by arrangement with Jane's Publishing Company Limited, London p. 21 Archives of Ontario p. 23, Photo by Gauvin & Gentzel Halifax Jan. 10, 1918, Nova Scotia Museum file P17/26.41, copy negative N-5278 p. 26, Courtesy of the Halifax Herald Limited, Halifax p. 27,45,50,51, Photograph Collection Public Archives of Nova Scotia p. 28, Public Archives of Nova Scotia p. 30, Photograph Collection Public Archives of Nova Scotia p. 31, Photograph Collection Public Archives of Nova Scotia p. 34, City of Toronto Archives SC 244 James Collection # 2435 p. 35, NAC C 17501 p. 36, City of Toronto Archives James Collection # 2441 p. 38, Photograph Collection Public Archives of Nova Scotia p. 39, NAC C 130352 p. 41, Photograph Collection Public Archives of Nova Scotia p. 42, Photograph Collection Public Archives of Nova Scotia p. 43, City of Toronto Archives James Collection # 2448 p. 44, NAC PA 22744 p. 44, City of Toronto Archives James Collection SC 244 # 1782 p. 50, City of Toronto Archives James Collection # 1788 p. 47, National Archives of Canada, Fred Longland Papers, MG 30, E 183 p. 51, Photograph Collection Public Archives of Nova Scotia p. 52, City of Toronto Archives SC 244 James Collection # 2456 p. 53, University Archives Killam Memorial Library Dalhousie University Halifax Nova Scotia p. 54 Photos by Joan Roue Dartmouth Nova Scotiap. 56, Photos by Nicholson Archives Burnaby Ont., p. 57, City of Toronto Archives James Collection # 2458 p. 62. Silhouette reproduced from The Steel Navy by James Dolby (MacDonald, London 1962).